LIVING TOGETHER AFTER RETIREMENT
THE SECOND EDITION!

by Graham Harrop

ISBN: 9781078204729

for Pamela

I don't CARE what she told you ... I'm watching the Kentucky Derby and the storm windows can wait!

My wife and I are spending far too much time together since I retired. Tonight's my turn to hide behind the chesterfield.

Let me know if this bothers you...

My wife and I are on a road trip. I'll need earplugs, aspirin and one of those 'Keep Smilin'!' stickers.

I can only fix a pain in the butt if it's your own. I can't do anything if it's your husband.

It's a hundred bucks to write: 'Yes-
I've taken my vitamins!' and another
fifty to write: 'Get off my back!'

**It's an ultimatum from Mother.
Either you go or she does.**

It could be age or it could be the ten years that you spent on the road with the Grateful Dead.

You've really got to get out more.

I'm not getting the sleep that I should. Tell me again what happened at the nail salon.

It'd be a heck of a lot easier if you'd just get your flu shot!

The chiropractor wants to know why you used a six iron instead of a five on that hole...

Did you send away for an: *'Own your own desert island!'* brochure'?

Has your: 'Friends of the Neighbourhood' group gone?

I don't have any ailments. I just thought I'd stick around in case anything went wrong.

Would it kill you to take him to the dog park?

**It's a special dietary request.
If they don't have Heineken, get Coors.**

You're spending far too much time here, Walter!

You lost the little notebook that I gave you, didn't you?

It's just until we get the cough suppresant!

First you tell me to wash the kitchen floor, and then you change your mind!

I told you what would happen if you left your dirty clothes in the bathroom one more time, didn't I?

Since when did the 'to do' list become the 'to don't' list, and why is my Kirk Douglas impression on it?

You can watch the Stanley Cup Finals anytime - kitty and I want to watch the Louisiana Sewing Bee!

According to my calculations, if we manage our savings prudently and wisely, we'll have enough money to last until next Thursday.

It activates if you leave the toilet seat up!

My name's Rose and I'll be your waitress. Can I start you off with the half-eaten muffin that you left on the counter last night?

You're spending far too much time on that park bench!

Well? Are you coming in or not?

They were out of miniature submarines so I got you Captain Kelp and Bubble Man.

Well? Did you find the remote?

So you want 'Happy Birthday, Harold!' in big letters and 'Quit scratching your butt!' in smaller ones.

It's your pharmacist. He wants to know if you'll be driving any heavy machinery in the next 24 hours.

You and your wife still not speaking?

For your information, it's called remodeling and it saves a hell of a lot of time getting to the kitchen!

What do you mean you're not in...

There! You see? Grocery shopping isn't as much fun as you thought, now, is it?

I get bored, too, you know!

I HEARD YOU THE FIRST TIME!

The dog wants to play golf ...

Made in United States
North Haven, CT
18 July 2024

55089807R10029